What pe say......

I laughed until my q_x became 1.
R-punzel

I'd break into a house to read this book.
Goldilocks

I ate this book up in one go!
The Big Bad Wolf

Zzzz...
Sleeping Actuary

Actuarial Fairy Tales

Other books
by the author

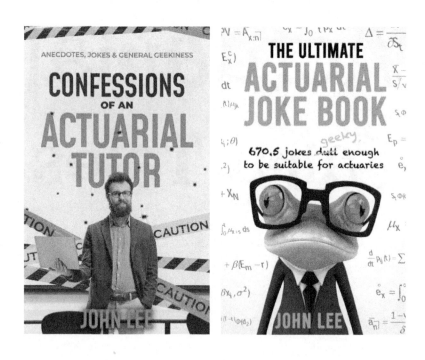

Actuarial/mathematical/Excel memes/jokes
www.actuarialtutor.substack.com

Actuarial Fairy Tales

Statistically Significant Stories

John Lee

Published by:

Kingdom Collective Publishing
KCP

Unit 10936, PO Box 6945

London, W1A 6US

kingdomcollectivepublishing@gmail.com

Book and Cover idea by John Lee, design by 100covers

ISBN: 978-1-912045-18-1

First Edition: December 2021

Dedication

This one's for all my friends.

At least it will be when I find some.

Acknowledgements

Many thanks once again to my brave beta readers who selflessly expose themselves to the risk of reading my first draft. All so that you, dear reader, are protected from the consequences of my unrefined humour, especially as no insurance company offers coverage against the lower tail of John's jokes.

Greg Solomon, Emma Wang, Jordan Chong, Kanishka Singhal, CATuary (@Catuary1), Raquel Stokes, Adam Biros, Shaikh Mujtaba Ali, David Yardley, Dave Johnson, Leigh Costanza, Sam Naude and Sam Mawoyo.

Contents

Once Upon a Time...

There lived a beautiful dataset and their handsome assumptions.

Constructing an Actuarial Fairy Tale Model

As with all actuarial models, I first set about gathering data by conducting a thorough internet search for fairy tales. Well, at least the first page of results, anyway.

I then threw out the obvious outliers in the data, like the king who wished to marry his daughter (weird) and Bluebeard, who kills all his wives (rather dark).

Then I cleaned the data, removing some of the less salient details from Cinderella (like chopping off parts of their feet to fit in the glass shoe) and Sleeping Beauty (let's just say the kiss version is much better than Giambattista Basile's original).

Using the principle of parsimony, I found using only a one-joke factor model would provide an adequate fit to create a funny story as actuaries have a low bar for humour.

Next, I used this same joke in a variety of fairy tales to ensure there was enough diversification to reduce the specific risk of readers not finding this book funny.

However, despite this, the systematic risk that actuaries don't have any sense of humour in the first place remains.

The Fairy Tale Models

Traditional tales with an actuarial twist.

Little Red-Eyed Riding Actuary

Data source

https://www.worldoftales.com/European_folktales/
English_folktale_116.html

Assumptions underlying this fairy tale model

- Wolves can talk and are pretty good at mimicry.

- Actuaries engage in conversation with strangers, even if those strangers are talking wolves.

- Wolves are frightened of actuarial recruiters.

- Wolves are able to swallow people whole.

- Actuaries do not induce vomiting when eaten.

- A wolf's stomach can stretch enough to fit two people ("best fit").

- The aforementioned swallowed people don't die.

- Actuarial recruiters are skilled in the use of axes.

Once upon a timeline, in a life insurer's office, there worked an actuarial intern. She was called "Little Red-Eyed Riding Actuary" because she was new and worked so many hours to please her team that she had bloodshot eyes.

One day her manager, having heard her grandma was ill, said to her, "Go see how your grandmother is doing, for I hear that her force of mortality is increasing exponentially. This may be the ideal opportunity to see if she's interested in buying some long-term care or critical illness cover funded by an equity release."

Little Red-Eyed Riding Actuary set out immediately to go to her grandmother, who lived in another village.

As she was walking through the woods, she met a wolf who wanted to eat her up, but he dared not because some actuarial recruiters had already latched onto the scent of Little Red Eyed Riding Actuary and were closing in.

The wolf asked her where she was going. The young actuary did not realise that it was dangerous to engage in small talk with anyone, let alone wolves. For, if she'd carried out some basic exploratory data analysis of fairy tales, she would have quickly discovered that wolves are statistically very likely to be the villains of the story.

"I am going to see if grandmother is interested in purchasing long-term care or critical life cover."

"Does she live far off?" asked the wolf.

"It is the first house on the right beyond the mill," answered Little Red-Eyed Riding Actuary, breaching GDPR.

Now Little Red-Eyed Riding Actuary had calculated the quickest route to get there, considering the effect of the rising terrain on her rate of walking. However, the wolf pointed out to her that loggers had been working on a different path and she would maximise her *log*-likelihood of getting there if she were to take it.

This seemed sensible to the girl, and she took that path while the wolf ran as fast as he could along the shortest route to the grandmother's house and knocked on the door.

"Who's there?"

"Your grandchild," replied the wolf, trying hard to make his voice sound boring enough to be mistaken for an actuary.

"Lift the latch," called out the grandmother, "I am in a morbid state, and cannot get up."

The wolf lifted the latch; sprang in and ate her up in one bite. He then shut the door, dressed himself in her nightcap, got into the grandmother's bed, and used a constant arrival rate assumption to model the waiting time before Little Red-Eyed

Riding Actuary knocked at the door.

"Who's there?"

Little Red-Eyed Riding Actuary was at first concerned upon hearing the deep voice of the wolf, but then realised that 95% of ill people's hoarse voice confidence intervals would still include this sound.

She answered, "It is your grandchild, Little Red-Eyed Riding Actuary."

The wolf softened his voice as much as he could and said, "Lift the latch and come in."

When Little Red-Eyed Riding Actuary came in, she saw her grandmother lying in bed with her cap pulled far over her face, and looking like a definite outlier to the Grandmother's appearance distribution.

Nevertheless, she started with a null hypothesis that it was indeed her grandmother and carried out a test based on a sample of her grandmother's appearance.

"Oh grandmother," she said, "What big ears you have!"

"All the better to hear you say that I'm still within three standard deviations of the mean, my child."

"But, grandmother, what significantly big eyes you have!"

"All the better to see that a sample size of only one grandma means your standard error is too large to draw any conclusion, my child."

"But, grandmother, what a big chamber pot you have!"

"All the better for my large p-value, my child."

"Oh! But, grandmother, what big teeth you have!"

"All the better to shred any 'correlation is causation' arguments you may have."

And so Little Red-Eyed Riding Actuary became convinced that she had insufficient evidence to reject her null hypothesis at the 5% level. But then she noticed the fat tail distribution of her grandmother and gasped, "Oh! But, grandmother, what a significantly big tail weight you have!"

And realising that his game was up, the wolf swallowed up Little Red-Eyed Riding Actuary in one gulp!

"I appear to have made a Type 2 error," sighed Little Red-Eyed Riding Actuary from within the wolf's stomach and vowed never to talk to strangers again.

Now the wolf was feeling quite nauseous after eating the bland actuary, for she was not as good to eat as his tastiness model had predicted. So he lay down again in the bed whilst he updated his model, but instead fell asleep, and began to snore loudly.

An actuarial recruiter who was "just passing" the house looking for someone, literally anyone, to fill a post, heard the snoring and went in. The recruiter discounted the strange appearance of the grandmother at a rate of 5% *pa* because he got his commission, regardless. However, when the recruiter noticed the posterior distribution of the wolf's belly, he used an axe to split the wolf into its principal components.

Little Red-Eyed Riding Actuary was so grateful to be alive and desirous to do a more boringly safe job, she readily accepted the position offered by the recruiter.

The grandmother now realised the importance of life cover and purchased every product available from the actuary.

And the Profession was delighted as they could now collect another year's worth of membership fees from Little Red-Eyed Riding Actuary.

Goldilocks and the 3 Bear market Analysts

Data source

https://www.worldoftales.com/European_folktales/
English_folktale_18.html

Assumptions

- It is possible to lock spreadsheets with special gold locks for added security (and style).

- Actuaries go for walks in the woods (even if those woods are, shockingly, outside of their office).

- Market analysts purchase office insurance and go for walks when their models are processing.

- Actuaries prefer less company to more.

- Actuaries routinely collect assumptions and models wherever they might find them.

- Actuaries can run away when the need arises.

Once upon a stock market, there were three analysts who worked together in an office in a wood. Now all three of them were predicting a bear market; the first analyst was predicting a small bear market – more of a minor blip, really. The second analyst was predicting a middle-sized bear market – a slump, to be sure. And the final analyst was predicting a huge bear market – a stock-market crash.

One day, after they had constructed their trend forecast models for breakfast and set them to run, they went for a walk in the woods while the models were processing.

While they were out walking, a little actuary came upon their office. She was called Goldilocks because she always used gold locks on her spreadsheets so that no-one could ever edit them.

She could not have been following the actuaries' code of conduct because she looked in the window and, seeing nobody in the office, she calculated that the occupancy probability was near zero and she lifted the latch.

The door was not locked, because the market analysts had insurance. This was a classic example of moral hazard.

Though to be fair, the analysts believed that, according to the efficient market hypothesis, all available information (such as the chance of strangers breaking into their office) was included in their stock prices.

So Goldilocks went inside; which would make her seem like a risk-seeking actuary (an oxymoron, to be sure). However, in her defence, the office was less crowded than the woods at that moment and so it was the logical choice for any introverted actuary to make.

When she saw the forecasting models processing on the table, she thought she'd maximise her return given the risk she'd already taken entering the office by using Mean-Variance Portfolio Theory (MVPT).

First, she examined the assumptions of the analyst who was predicting a huge bear market, and they were too prudent. Then she examined the assumptions of the analyst who was predicting a small bear market, and they were too weak. And finally she examined the assumptions of the analyst who was predicting a middle-sized bear market; and they were neither too prudent nor too weak, but just right best estimate assumptions; and she liked them so well that she took the paper they were written on.

Next, she inspected the number of parameters used by the analyst who was predicting a huge bear market, and they were too many. Then she inspected the number of parameters used by the analyst who was predicting a small bear market, and they were too few. And finally she inspected the number of parameters used by the analyst who was predicting a middle-sized bear market; and they were neither too many nor too few, but just right as they minimised Akaike's Information Criterion (AIC); and she liked them so well that she also took this paper they were written on.

Then Goldilocks checked the laptop that was processing the stochastic model for the analyst who was predicting a huge bear market, and it was running too many simulations and would not finish processing for another week. Then she checked the laptop that had long since finished processing the deterministic model for the analyst who was predicting a small bear market, and it was using too few scenarios. And finally, she checked the laptop that had just finished processing the model for the analyst who was predicting a middle-sized bear market; and they were neither too many simulations nor too few, but 1,000 just right scenarios selected via importance sampling; and she liked them so well that she also took the laptop.

By this time, the three bear market analysts thought their models would have finished processing (though one of them was clearly being wildly optimistic) and so they headed back to the office.

```
size = {huge, small, medium}

item = {assumptions, parameters, simulations}
```

```
For i = 1 to 3

    For j = 1 to 3

        The  analyst  who  was  predicting  the
        <size j> bear market said "Who's been
        fiddling with my <item i>?"
```

By the time the analysts finished these loops, they had discovered Goldilocks holding the papers and the laptop.

Now, despite normally being passive investors, they became actively threatening and executed a short tactical asset re-allocation and soon had the stolen items back.

Goldilocks ran away as fast as her legs could carry her. Though, to be fair, her speed was more due to fear of being near other people rather than fear of getting caught.

Fortunately, the three bear market analysts' insurance covered any damages caused by actuaries (both physical and psychological) despite them leaving doors unlocked. Possibly because this is a fairy tale and not real life.

And the three analysts never saw anything more of Goldilocks; which is just as it should be with all actuaries.

Hansel & Gumbel

Data source

https://www.worldoftales.com/fairy_tales/Brothers_Grimm/
Margaret_Hunt/Hansel_and_Grethel.html

Assumptions

- There is a market for woodcutter personal accident cover.

- There is a high concentration of 1 in 200 year events in the short timeline of this story.

- Actuaries can be made to go for random walks in forests.

- ~~Accountants~~ witches often build houses made of food in forests to lure in lost actuaries.

- ~~Accountants~~ witches have a strong enough constitution that they can stomach eating actuaries.

- The correct path out of the forest can be found by repeated iterations before the end of this story.

- Readers who prefer mathematics to reading can cope with a longer story.

Once upon a stochastic process there dwelt on the outskirts of a large forest a poor woodcutter insurance CEO with his CFO and two trainee actuaries; the boy was called Hansel and the girl Gumbel. Demand for woodcutter personal accident and sickness cover was scant enough, but then there was a great recession and the CEO couldn't even provide the trainee actuaries with headed notepaper and mechanical pencils.

One late night, as he was examining the latest terrible projections, he sighed and said to his CFO: "What's to become of our company? How are we to support our expensive trainees and their study support packages, now that we have nothing more for ourselves?"

"I'll tell you what, boss," answered the CFO; "early tomorrow morning we'll take the trainees out on a ramble through the actuarial countryside; there we shall give them each some reserve calculations to work on; then we'll go do our work and leave them behind. Since actuaries rarely leave the office, they won't have a hope of finding their way back, and we shall thus be rid of them without having to pay severance."

"No, my CFO," said her boss, "that I won't do; how could I find it in my heart to sell insurance without the due diligence performed by my actuaries? Besides, abandoning them outside will leave them at the mercy of conversation with strangers."

"Oh! You fool," said she, "you might just as well declare

bankruptcy," and she left him no peace till he consented.

"But I can't help feeling sorry for the poor (but not in a monetary sense) actuaries," sighed the CEO.

The trainee actuaries had been working late at the office, and overheard what their CFO had said to their CEO. Gumbel wept bitterly and spoke to Hansel: "I told you this tail event would occur"

"No, no, Gumbel," said Hansel, "don't assume the worst outcome; I'll be able to mitigate this risk, have no fear."

At first he thought about taking out "getting lost in the woods" insurance – but these policies were currently over-valued and there was no way he was going to pay more than the fair price. Besides, if they actually became lost in the woods, how would they ever be able to contact the insurer to make a claim, since mobile phones hadn't been invented yet?

He then settled on avoiding the risk by refusing to go outside the office, but should that fail, he would reduce the risk of becoming lost by leaving a trail of pages from The Actuary magazine to follow back to the office.

At daybreak, even before the sun was up, the CFO came and woke the two actuaries: "Get up; we're all going to the forest to sell insurance."

"You don't need us," replied Hansel.

However, the CFO easily overcame their avoidance mitigation approach by luring them away from their desks with the promise of a shiny new Excel macro, which would be useful when Excel would be finally released in 1987 (some 175 years[1] from now).

They initiated a simple random walk, and it was indeed random as the CEO flipped an unbiased coin to decide which path to take at each junction.

However, Hansel reduced the risk of becoming lost by dropping pages of The Actuary magazine out of his (rather large) pocket on to the path.

When they had reached the middle of the forest, the CEO said, "Now, go calculate some premiums and I'll find some woodcutters to be our customers."

The CFO added: "After all, we know how much you hate small talk, so just stay here while we go selling and when we've finished, we'll come back and fetch you."

Hansel and Gumbel sat down and ran calculations for the

---

1 Given how valuable Excel will be to actuaries, its present value, even discounted back 175 years, is still enough to lure any actuary away into the woods.

longest time until their eyes closed with fatigue, and they fell fast asleep, because coffee and energy drinks had also not been invented yet. When they awoke at last, it was pitch dark.

Gumbel began to cry, "I told you that this catastrophe would occur. Now how will we ever to get out of this wood?"

But Hansel comforted her. "Wait a bit," he said, "till the moon is up, and then you'll see that my risk management technique won't have let us down."

And when the moon had risen, they followed the glossy pages, which shone like freshly polished F9 keys, all the way back to the office.

The CFO opened the door and shouted, "You filthy actuaries, sleeping on the job in the woods!" For she never much liked actuaries who always seemed to be too clever by far.

But the CEO rejoiced, for his ~~regulator~~ conscience had reproached him for selling insurance without an actuary to sign off on his reserves[2].

---

2 Bizarrely, this story skips how the company survived. So let's assume that the recession led many woodcutters to take out personal accident cover, thinking to remove a limb or two should things become too dire. Then there was a rather unexpected cold snap which drove up demand for wood. Thus, the woodcutters never claimed on their policies, leading to a healthy profit margin for the company.

However, not long afterward there was yet another 1 in 200 year recession, and the CFO spoke to the CEO late one night: "We've drained the company accounts dry. The actuaries must be got rid of! We'll use a *general* random walk this time, so that they definitely won't be able to find their way out of the forest again. There's simply no other way of saving ourselves."

The CEO's heart weighed on him heavily, and he thought: "Surely it would be better to go down with one's actuaries for they are the backbone of the insurance business!" But his CFO wouldn't listen to his arguments, and did nothing but scold and reproach him until he gave in a second time.

But the actuaries were again working late in the office (because they had no real life outside of it) and had heard the whole conversation. When the CEO and CFO had departed for the night, Hansel went to fetch magazines for his tried and tested risk mitigation strategy; but the CFO had learned from her mistake and locked the cupboards and barred the outside door to prevent any operational risks from upsetting her plans. But Hansel consoled his fellow actuary, and said: "Don't cry, Gumbel, for I will use Google maps to reduce the risk of us getting lost tomorrow."

"What is Google maps?" she responded.

It was then that Hansel realised his plan lacked one important element. "Change of plan – I'll use this mouldy loaf that someone left in the fridge to leave a trail to remove the risk of us getting lost."

Gumbel was little consoled, for she realised that the prevalence of these so called "1 in 200 year events" could only be explained by a copula and hence worse was likely to occur.

At dawn, the CFO unlocked the office and led the actuaries on a general random walk into the woods. Hansel crumbled the bread in his pocket, and every few minutes he stood still and dropped a crumb on the ground. "Hansel, what are you stopping and looking about you for?" said the CEO.

"I'm looking for my... err... personality," answered Hansel.

"Fool!" said the CFO; "everyone knows you two became actuaries because you didn't have the personalities to be accountants!"

The CFO led them deeper into the forest; further than they had ever been in their lives before. Which for actuaries who live at the office, wasn't really saying all that much.

Then they were told to sit and calculate reserves, while the senior management went into the forest to sell policies. "When we've met our quota, we'll come back to fetch you."

The actuaries kept working for hours and evening passed away, but nobody came to get them. It was only when they couldn't perform any more calculations; that they realised it was pitch dark.

Gumbel lectured Hansel about properly modelling tail events, but Hansel replied, "Worry not, just wait till the moon rises, then we shall see the breadcrumbs I scattered along the path which will show us the way back to the office."

When the moon appeared they got up, but they found no crumbs, for the birds had picked them all up.

"Now our dataset is censored, we risk never finding our way home *and* getting eaten by a witch too," cried Gumbel.

"You really need to stop overstating tail events, Gumbel," replied Hansel. "All is not lost, for birds eating breadcrumbs is *informative* censoring."

"What does it tell us?" asked Gumbel hopefully.

"That the birds are *more* hungry than us. Now let's examine the risk vs. return of our present situation."

"More like risk vs. not returning," wailed Gumbel.

"We shall share the risk of becoming lost between us – which already reduces it by half for each of us! Next, all we have to do to find the way back to the office is to eliminate every wrong path. It should take only a couple of hours to run such a simple machine learning algorithm on my laptop."

"What's a laptop?" enquired Gumbel.

It was then that Hansel realised his plan lacked one important element. "Never mind," said Hansel, "we'll just run the algorithm manually. We'll be fine as long as we don't starve before we've tried every path."

Despite Hansel's excellent plan, he was confused why Gumbel was little consoled. They wandered about the entire night, and the next day and...

```
for i = 1 to (number of paths)

    if path i leads to the office or
    somewhere interesting

    then stop

    otherwise repeat
```

Eventually, on iteration number 493, they came to a cottage made of bread and roofed with cakes, with windows made of transparent sugar. Hansel immediately began to eat, but Gumbel warned him, "Shouldn't we consider the occupancy probability of the cottage before consuming it?"

But Hansel ignored her, so Gumbel had no choice but to report him to the Profession for breaking the actuaries' code as his hunger had clearly compromised his professional judgement.

Suddenly, the door opened, and an ancient dame leaning on a

staff hobbled out. Hansel and Gumbel were terrified but the old woman shook her head and said: "My dear actuaries, I have some gifts for you – come in and calculate their worth."

Hansel and Gumbel couldn't resist the opportunity to calculate some present values and thus they were lured in by the old woman who really was ~~an accountant~~ a witch that took pleasure in eating actuaries.

So it was that Hansel became locked in a little stable to be fattened up before becoming the ~~accountant's~~ witch's dinner.

"I'm sorry Gumbel," apologised Hansel, "I should have listened to you! I wrongly assumed that extreme events are independent."

"That's what everybody says until these tail events actually occur," replied Gumbel. "But on the bright side you're now a *captive insurer* that can provide a payment during this extreme event."

And so they knew that at least their monetary problems were over.

Now witches have red eyes, and cannot see far, but they have a keen sense of smell (which can sniff out dodgy accounts up to 100 metres away). Thus, it was that she mistakenly locked Hansel away when Gumbel clearly had a fatter tail.

So came the day when the old dame was ready to eat them, though she had drunk far too much whiskey the night before and had a terrible ANOVA.

"I've heated the oven and kneaded the dough," said the witch to Gumbel. "Now crawl into the oven and audit whether it's properly heated for the bread." For she meant to close the oven once Gumbel was inside so that she might eat her up too.

But Gumbel linearly extrapolated her true intention, and employed a risk transfer technique by saying: "I don't know how I'm to do it; how exactly do I get in?"

"You silly actuary with no practical skills!" said the hag, "the opening is big enough for even me to fit in," and she poked her head into the oven to demonstrate.

Then Gumbel gave the witch a shove that sent her right in, so the witch's hypothesis might be properly tested. Then she shut the iron door, drew the bolt and concluded that the oven was indeed big enough.

Gumbel opened the little stable door, and cried: "Hansel, we are risk-free; the old woman is dead, and what's more, she had life insurance!" They hugged one another with relief and then, shocked at their display of emotion; they quickly apologised and went back to behaving like proper actuaries.

"But now," said Hansel, "let's continue with our algorithm and find our way back to the office."

So it was only after 7,892 more iterations, they saw the office again and were reunited with their CEO, but this time they were careful to keep their emotions in check.

The poor man had not been able to conduct business since the regulators closed him down and the CFO had quit. But once Gumbel deposited the two insurance payments, their company met the minimum capital requirements and soon the actuaries were able to change the world for the better, one personal woodcutter accident policy at a time.

And the CEO let the actuaries live permanently at the office so they never had to go outside ever again.

The Magic Actuarial Recruiter Pot

Data source

https://www.worldoftales.com/fairy_tales/Brothers_Grimm/
Margaret_Hunt/Sweet_Porridge.html

Assumptions

- The reader is based in a country where there is a shortage of actuaries, so that jokes about pushy actuarial recruiters are funny.

- Old actuarial recruiters lurk in forests.

- The little actuarial trainee's mother did not instruct her to be wary of actuarial recruiters in forests.

- It is asymptotically possible to stop the flow of emails, phone calls and so on from actuarial recruiters. Though it may need to involve the use of magic.

Once there was a little pensions actuarial trainee who lived alone with her mother (for she had no friends), and she lived from valuation to valuation.

Some would say she was rich while others would say she suffered from personality poverty. Either way, she longed for something more than her endless reviewing, and wondered whether her life might be sweeter if she got another actuarial job.

So the trainee went into the actuarial job forest, and there she met an aged recruiter woman who could sense her ~~naivety~~ sorrow, and presented her with a little magic actuarial recruiter pot. The recruiter told her that when the words "Recruit, little pot, recruit" were spoken, the pot would send her details about good, sweet actuarial jobs.

The girl took the pot home to her mother, overjoyed that this would soon free them from the need to work all hours to complete those valuations, for they would now receive details of job opportunities as often as they chose.

Sadly, though, the little pot could not deliver the actuary from her lack of friends, as that is beyond the power of actuarial recruiter magic.

Straight away the girl said to the magic pot, "Recruit, little pot, recruit". Immediately, she started receiving emails and phone calls about many job openings with "competitive salaries" that were "just perfect" for her. She listened to all the sweet words of the recruiters who were "blown away" by her résumé until she was satisfied (well, until she got bored with all the fawning and stopped listening).

However, soon she became overwhelmed with more offers than she could ever want (and many more that she didn't want) and so she sought to stop the magic actuarial recruiter pot from sending any more emails, phone calls, smoke signals, faxes and even letters. But only then did she realise that the aged recruiter woman had never told her how to stop the pot!

First, she tried saying "Stop, little pot, stop" but this had no effect on the torrent of messages. Next she tried replies of "I love my current role and am not interested in other jobs at the moment," but alas, it was to no avail. It was almost like they weren't even listening to her.

So she tried unsubscribing from their "update" emails, then when that didn't work she reported them as spam, but still they kept on coming. In the end, she resorted to blocking them, but for every company she blocked, another two would start messaging her until her inbox reached its storage limit.

In addition, her voicemail became full, and she had to screen every call to her mobile, home phone and work phone to prevent any more "I'm just wondering if you're interested in..."

conversations.

But then she started getting LinkedIn messages, friend requests on Facebook and recruiters sliding in to her DMs on Twitter, Instagram and TikTok. Even deleting her social media accounts wasn't enough – for they started turning up to her house in person and asking the same questions.

Other recruiters rented properties in her street and "accidentally" bumped into her as she left the house. One committed recruiter even married into her family and so she was no longer safe from being asked about job openings at family events.

There was only one way out that she could see – to fake her own death. The medication that she took made her appear dead for 24 hours, which meant she mercifully missed all the recruiters at her funeral share how sad it was that someone who was such a perfect fit for their job had been cruelly taken away from them.

As planned, she awoke in the coffin in the grave, but before they had filled it in. However, she suddenly noticed how crowded it was in the coffin. "I didn't think I'd be this claustrophobic," she murmured to herself.

"You're alive!" whispered an excited voice.

"Who's there?" screamed the terrified actuary, kicking away

from what she had thought was the side of the coffin.

"I'm Richard, from Recruit-me-quick. I knew I was right not to give up hope even if it meant being buried alive with you!"

It was at this point of desperation that the poor little actuary finally broke...

"OK, I'll do it!"

"You will? Fantastic!" replied the recruiter, delighted that his dedication to the cause had finally paid off.

"... for half of your commission."

"Sorry?"

"Well, by accepting this job I'm helping you out, so it seems only fair that I receive some remuneration as part of the deal."

The recruiter was speechless and said nothing at all, because that's what being speechless means. Instead, he made a panicked escape from the coffin and set a new Olympic record for the 200m sprint.

Word soon spread through the actuarial recruiter community that she would cost them money, and the little actuary became blacklisted and never heard from any recruiter ever again.

And she lived as happily ever after as any actuary with no friends and no life outside of the office could.

Sleeping Actuary

Data source

https://www.worldoftales.com/fairy_tales/
Andrew_Lang_fairy_books/Blue_fairy_book/
The_Sleeping_Beauty_in_the_Wood.html

Data cleaning

The whole ogre mother-in-law thing was removed, as it was a clear outlier to the pleasant story remembered by most people.

Assumptions

- There exist actuarial and accounting fairies that have the power to bless or curse.

- No risk mitigation technique can completely undo a curse from an accounting fairy.

- Actuaries are powerless to resist the lure of Excel, even if their life is at risk.

Once upon a mortality curve, there lived a king and queen who had fallen on hard times, for they had no children and this grieved them very much indeed so that they spent all their money drowning their sorrows in a sea of wine and Netflix.

But one day, as the queen was walking, she saw a poor little actuary that had accidentally taken a wrong turn and had stumbled into the outside world. The actuary was paralysed with fear and stood gasping, not knowing what to do. The queen took pity on the actuary and had the streets cleared of people. The actuary regained his composure and safely returned to his office to do more work.

A day later, the queen received an email from the actuary saying, "Thank you for your help, kind queen. In return I have carried out extensive modelling to find the best way to maximise the chance of you having the child you seek."

The queen followed the actuary's recommendation and soon gave birth to a little girl. The king was so delighted that he took out a loan to hold a grand feast to make merry and show the child to all the land. The queen said, "I will have the fairies attend so that they might bestow mathematical genius upon our little daughter, then she might grow up and become an actuary." For the queen had heard that the actuaries received a generous pay package which would solve all their financial worries.

So seven actuarial fairies came and when the feasting was over, they gathered round and gave their best gifts to the little princess. One gave her mathematical ability, another gave a set of actuarial tables that would constantly update in real time, another gave her many exemptions from the actuarial exams so her personality would not be destroyed, and so on until she had all that a good actuary should ever want.

However, just as six of them had finished blessing her, the door to the hall slammed open and in walked the accounting fairy full of resentment, for the queen had not invited her for fear of upsetting the actuarial fairies. Also, she despised actuaries because they thought they were superior, since they used more than just addition and subtraction to do... erm... something... er... complicated.

So she set to work to take her revenge and declared: "The king's daughter shall, during the accident hump in her fifteenth year, experiment with Excel and cause a circular error and thus die of shock."

Then the seventh actuarial fairy who had not yet given her gift came forward and said, "Fear not, O king and queen, for I shall use my blessing to mitigate this mortality risk. Whilst your daughter shall cause Excel to have a circular error, instead of dying of shock, she shall only fall into a deep slumber which shall have an expected future sleep time of 100 years."

However, the king was unimpressed by this risk mitigation, as he desperately needed his daughter's actuarial salary to pay off the debt he had accrued. So he ordered that Excel should be deleted from every computer in the land and he forbade stores from ever selling it.

There was a great outcry from the actuaries and accountants who had to return to the "dark ages" of pencil and paper. But despite this, all the gifts from the six fairies came true, and the princess became known throughout the land as a mathematical prodigy and by twelve, she was already offering consultancy services to the insurance industry.

But one day when she was fifteen years old, the young princess was lost in thought over how crane fly (aka Daddy Longlegs) insurance could be profitable given their proclivity for losing legs, when she found herself by an unfamiliar door.

In the door there was a golden key, and shocked by her own risk-seeking impulse, she turned the key and stepped inside to see the most wondrous site. An old woman working on a computer program with grids that were being used for producing reams and reams of numbers with a speed that the princess had never witnessed before. "What a beautiful program," said the princess, "that would simply revolutionise my work."

"It's called Excel," explained the old lady, "you can program it with formulae to carry out multiple calculations at once. Would you like to try?"

The princess was delighted to try it out and quickly discovered goal seek. "I could use this to optimise model parameters!" "Ah yes," said the old lady, "I use Gompertz' Law to model the exponentially increasing mortality rate – it doesn't matter how hard you try, you just can't escape it."

Scarcely had the old dame said this before the fairy's prophecy was fulfilled; Excel threw a circular error, and the princess died of shock.

The old woman cried out for help and people came in from every quarter in great numbers. They tried to revive her by shouting, throwing water on her face and even threatening to mess up her tidy desk; but nothing would bring her to herself. It was probably a good thing too, as the actuarial princess would have been horrified to be in such close proximity to so many people.

However, she was not dead, but had only fallen into a deep sleep; kind of like actuarial students do after an exam season. And now the king, who came up at the noise, saw that what the fairies had decreed passed. So he had the princess carried into the finest apartment in his palace, and to be laid upon a bed with her actuarial tables and the Excel file placed beside her.

The king commanded they should not disturb her, but leave the palace and let her slumber until her future expected sleep time had passed.

And as they left the palace, Brownian motion set to work and within an hour's time there had grown up around the palace such a vast number of trees, great and small, bushes and brambles, twining one within another, that neither man nor beast nor examiner nor actuarial recruiter nor even someone from work asking if she could just come in to help them finish a project before the urgent deadline could pass.

After many years, there came to that land the prince of loss adjusters investigating suspicious claims. He interviewed an old actuary who shared the story of the thicket of thorns; and how a beautiful palace stood behind it, where a wonderful actuarial princess lay in it asleep. The old man shared how many people from their office had tried to break through the thicket to seek her help, but they had all got stuck and died.

"Even the Profession has given up trying to get their annual fees," laughed the old man.

"Asleep, you say, and not dead?" inquired the loss adjuster.

"Well, she would have been dead had the fairy who cursed her to die on her fifteenth birthday had her way. But another fairy changed it to sleep."

"That is most interesting, thank you," replied the loss adjuster. His mind was wondering if there was a correlation between this story and the massive life insurance claim made by a king who now lived in the land across the sea.

Fired up, he headed towards the wood and despite the barriers; his coefficient of determination was so high that he soon made a straight line through the wood until at last he came upon the castle.

In no time, he found the chamber in which the princess lay and saw her beauty, her actuarial tables and the Excel file that had the circular error. However, he just couldn't take his eyes off of that circular error, and he knew he would not be at peace until he had found the problem and corrected it.

No sooner had he done so than the princess revived from her slumber and saw how the actuary had fixed the error, and she loved him. And at that moment, the prince of loss adjusters knew that the king's life insurance claim was void because not only was the princess not dead, but the king had neglected to mention the princess' pre-existing fairy condition.

But despite this, the two actuaries were married, and they lived as happily as two socially awkward people could together in the same house.

The Gingerbread Actuary

Data source

https://sites.pitt.edu/~dash/type2025.html

Assumptions

- Gingerbread can be used to create new actuarial students.

- It is possible (but with a probability of less than 0.01%) for actuaries to have personalities.

- Despite being stuck inside ovens for all of their life, new actuaries are fast runners and are able to purchase energy drinks.

- Short gingerbread legs can still outrun full-sized people.

- The existence of honorary fellowships of actuarial societies is ignored.

Once upon a continuous time set J, there lived two retired actuaries: a little old man and a little old woman in a little old house near the big old actuarial qualification river.

They would have been a very happy old couple, but for one thing: they'd never seen a qualified actuary with a personality, and so they wished for one very much.

One day, the little old woman took a random sample of gingerbread dough, rolled it flat and used a prior topological distribution to cut it into the shape of a mathematics graduate. She then added little triangles for feet and put it into the oven at all-or-nothing loss temperature.

When the posterior distribution of cooked dough was ready to be examined, the little old woman opened the oven door, but before she could find the Bayesian estimate, the gingerbread actuarial trainee jumped up and ran through the kitchen and out of the cottage, shouting, "You can't have my personality!"

The little old woman's credibility factor was zero until she realised she had given him run-off triangles for feet.

"Stop!" she yelled as she chased him. But the gingerbread actuary ran even faster, chanting, "Run, run, but you can't catch me. This actuary's got personality!"

The gingerbread actuary ran into his first job and passed the little old man whose interest was compounded continuously by the actuary's personality. "Stop," the little old man called out, "I want you to stay late at the office and finish this project for a client."

But the gingerbread actuary ran even faster, chanting, "I've run away from a little old woman, and I can run away from you too with 99% confidence. Run, run, but you can't catch me. This actuary's got personality!"

The little old man chased the gingerbread actuary, followed by the little old woman. But the gingerbread actuary ran significantly faster than them at the 1% level.

As the gingerbread actuary ran through late night working on his first job, he passed an actuarial recruiter. "Stop," the recruiter shouted, "I'd like to talk to you about some great opportunities that your personality is just perfect for."

But the gingerbread actuary ran even faster, chanting, "I've run from a little old woman and a little old man, and I can run away from you too.[3] Run, run, but you can't catch me. This actuary's got personality!"

---

[3] Which doesn't logically follow, as the recruiter was younger and so would be able to run faster than both the little old woman and little old man. But the gingerbread actuary was only a few minutes old and so presumably hadn't gathered enough data yet and hence his large standard error led him to erroneously make such a claim.

The recruiter chased the gingerbread actuary, followed by the little old woman and the little old man. But the gingerbread actuary ran significantly faster than them at the 3% level.

As the gingerbread actuary ran into new opportunities for promotion, he almost ran straight into the huge black beast of sleep deprivation. "Stop," the beast growled, "I want to leave you exhausted with no personality." But the gingerbread actuary drank Ye Olde Red Bull and ran even faster, chanting, "I've run from a little old woman and a little old man and a recruiter, and I can run away from you too as 'Ye Olde Red Bull gives you (dragon) wings'. Run, run, but you can't catch me. This actuary's got personality!"

The sleep deprivation beast chased the gingerbread actuary, followed by the recruiter and the little old woman and the little old man. But the gingerbread actuary ran significantly faster than them at the 5% level.

Finally, the gingerbread actuary reached the edge of the qualification river. It was too wide to jump, and sadly, the wings that Ye Olde Red Bull gives were only figurative. So the gingerbread actuary saw no option but to swim across, which would obviously get his personality wet and ruined.

A sly examiner fox saw the gingerbread actuary with personality and said, "Jump on my Financial Mathematics exam tail, and I'll take you across the qualification river!"

The gingerbread actuary thought to himself, "I'll be safe on his tail as it's an easy exam." So he jumped on and they started across the river.

Halfway across the river, the examiner barked, "Your personality's too heavy for my tail. Jump onto my Associate Exam back." So the gingerbread actuary smugly jumped on the examiner's back, thinking his personality would survive this journey easily.

Soon, the examiner fox said, "Your personality's too heavy for my back. Jump onto my Fellowship exam nose." So the gingerbread actuary jumped on the examiner's nose. But as soon as they reached the fully qualified riverbank, the examiner flipped the gingerbread actuary into the air, snapped his mouth shut, and began to eat the gingerbread actuary's personality up.

Presently the gingerbread actuary said, "Oh dear! My personality is quarter gone!" And soon, "Now it's three-quarters gone!" And then, "Using linear interpolation, it must have been half gone between my last two statements!"

And at last the gingerbread actuary cried out, "My personality's all gone!" and he never engaged in small talk again.

The Actuarial Princess and the p-Value

Data source

https://www.worldoftales.com/fairy_tales/
Hans_Christian_Andersen/Andersen_fairy_tale_47.html

Assumptions

- Princes and princesses can become actuaries and there exists at least one of each.

- Actuarial princesses go out for late night walks in storms.

- Only princesses wear princess dresses in storms.

- It is possible, through various statistical tests, to determine whether a princess is an actuarial princess at the 5% level.

Once upon a time series, there was an actuarial prince who wanted to marry a princess, but she must be an actuarial princess and not one who merely did data analysis.

So he travelled through the entire world to find one, but there was always something against each. Not that there was any lack of princesses, but none were truly actuarial princesses. For there was always something that caused him to reject them: whether it was their indifference to Excel, their lack of accuracy, or their outgoing personality. So he came home again in very low spirits (lower 0.5% tail), for he had very much wanted to marry an actuarial princess.

One night, there was a dreadful storm with thunder, lightning, and rain streaming down in torrents. It was easily a 1 in 200 year event. There was a knocking heard at the palace gate, and the old king went to open it.

There stood a princess outside the gate. At least the old king assumed she was a princess based on the assumption that only princesses wear princess dresses, which was a dodgy foundation, to be sure. But given that this fairy tale already had extremely rare storms and a king answering unannounced calls in the night instead of servants or guards, then what's a few more rare upper tail events between friends with a Gumbel copula?

Anyway, this (assumed) princess had water running down

from her hair and her dress into her shoes. Not from the storm, but from "working with a saturated model" so the actuarial princess claimed.

'We shall soon test that out!' thought the old queen, who was a dab hand at statistical analysis. Well, she had to be with her husband, who regularly made such dubious assumptions.

She started with the null hypothesis that the (assumed) princess was *not* an actuary, and after the princess had dried off, the queen arranged a little scenario analysis to test the princess's submitted claim. The queen invited the girl to a party to see how she'd cope with small talk.

The girl stood in a corner, staring at her feet, interacting only when someone asked her what she did for a living before the blank faces made her regret responding.

"Hmmm," thought the old queen, "she passed that test too easily. Let's see how she copes with a stress test…"

The old queen then debated what would be the most stressful event for a young actuary – having to explain a model's projections with someone repeatedly saying, "Sorry I don't understand. Can you explain that again?" Or maybe Excel throwing a circular reference error or just not responding before crashing?

However, in the end the queen, who had a bit of a sadistical statistical streak, had the poor girl work on a spreadsheet project where Excel was made to slow down to maximise the likelihood of inconvenience. Neither too little to be a minor annoyance, nor too much to allow the girl time to swap to another task. Just that perfect constant force of irritation.

Soon the girl was swearing in a most unprincess-like manner that just wouldn't be suitable for inclusion in this family friendly book.

"Well, it seems that she has passed that test too," muttered the old queen, "all that's left is a sensitivity test."

The old queen went into the princess' bedroom, took off all the bed-clothes, and laid a note saying "$\pi = 22/7$" on the bottom of the bed. However, unlike a rather similar fairy tale for non-actuarial audiences, she didn't pile multiple mattresses on top of the note, as that would increase the level/size of the bed test and thus make the result inconclusive. So instead she chose the smallest mattress for the bed in which the girl was to sleep and set about to examine the time series of her movements.

The next morning, the queen asked the princess how she had slept.

"Oh, very badly!" said the princess. "I just couldn't remain stationary all night! I don't know what was in the bed, but my whole body aches like it has been in the presence of a horrible inaccuracy!"

"Aha," thought the old queen, "since she wasn't stationary then they'll be some pattern to analyse with time series."

The old queen analysed whether the time series of the girl's positions throughout the night would conform to a random white noise process. But analysis of the turning points clearly showed that her movements were *not* random, with a p-value of less than 0.1%.

Now the queen perceived the princess was indeed an actuarial princess, because no one but an actuary could be so sensitive as to have such a small p-value (well apart from the 0.1% who aren't, but that would make a rather uncertain rubbish ending).

So the actuarial prince married her; for he knew now that at last he had got hold of a true actuarial princess.

And the p-values of these three tests were placed in a small Ljung-Box[4] in the Royal Museum, where it is still to be seen today.

---

[4] A Ljung-Box test is used to determine whether the residuals of a time series model are independent of each other. It's not actually a box you can store things in.

R-punzel

Data source

https://www.worldoftales.com/fairy_tales/
Andrew_Lang_fairy_books/Red_fairy_book/Rapunzel.html

Assumptions

- The reader knows that rampion is a European bellflower, with roots and leaves that can be used in salads.

- There exist at least two people who like the taste of rampion.

- Husbands asymptotically notice what their wives want as the number of hints approaches infinity.

- Witches who need to climb hair to get into tall towers can somehow get into that same tower in the first place without climbing hair to install someone with the hair they need to get there.

- Princes have a penchant for riding through forests and listening to singing about coding.

- The reader understands that the phrase "let down your hair" means to stop being so reserved, loosen up, and have fun.

Once upon a hazard function there lived a woman called Risk and her husband called Return. They were very unhappy because they had no actuarial child to help navigate the proper balance between them.

These good people (and they must have been good to desire to have an actuary as a child) had a little window at the back of their house, which looked into the most lovely garden, full of all manner of beautiful flowers and vegetables; but the garden was surrounded by a high wall, and no one dared to enter it, for it belonged to a witch of great power, who was feared by the whole world.

One day the woman stood at the window overlooking the garden, and saw there a bed full of the finest rampion: the leaves looked so fresh and green that she longed to eat them. Her risk appetite grew day by day because she longed for food that was extremely dangerous to get.

Her husband noticed (after his wife repeatedly dropped hints) and said: "What ails you, dear wife?"

"Oh," she answered as if surprised by his asking, "If I don't get some rampion to eat out of the garden behind the house, I know I shall die."

The man, who loved her dearly but was precise in his thinking, responded thus:

"You don't need rampion to know that you will die – for it is a certainty regardless of one's diet. Perhaps you meant dying early?"

The wife gave him *that* stare that only wives can.

He asked, "Have you carefully costed this project – what is the risk discount rate that you are using?"

"I am discounting all the risks, as it won't be me climbing over the wall into the garden..."

The husband thought to himself, "If only there were some kind of statutory controls to limit the risks a man is required to take to keep his wife happy."

However, since the payback period if he didn't do what his wife wanted could last several uncomfortable months, he dutifully climbed over the wall into the witch's garden at dusk, and, hastily gathered a handful of rampion leaves and returned with them to his wife. She made them into a salad, which tasted so good that her interest compounded for the forbidden food. This naturally required her husband to increase the risk that must be taken to get this higher return of rampion.

Since the husband's desire for a peaceful life meant the present value of no nagging was worth the risk taken, he climbed over the garden wall again at dusk to fetch her some more. But when he reached the other side, he drew back in terror, for standing before him was the old witch.

"How dare you," she said, with a wrathful glance, "climb into my garden and steal my rampion like a common thief? You shall suffer for your foolhardiness."

"Oh!" he implored, "pardon my presumption; but it was a quite sensible decision given that the net present value of my actions is positive at the weighted average cost of being berated for not meeting my wife's desire."

Then the witch's anger was a little appeased, and she said:

"If your calculations are as you say, then you may take as much rampion away with you as you like, but on one condition only: that you give me the actuarial child your wife will shortly bring into the world. All shall go well with it, and I will look after it as would a Trustee look after a pension scheme."

Since the husband only used a 10 day Value at Risk calculation, he did not properly consider the consequences of this long-tailed contingent liability (plus he didn't want to die right there and then) and so he foolishly agreed to everything she asked.

As soon as the actuarial child was born, the witch appeared and demanded the child. It was only then that the wife realised that exchange rate for rampion to child was rather penal and wished she had hedged this currency risk in her calculations. Having given the child the name of R-punzel, which was a sufficiently dour a name for an actuary, the witch carried the child off with her.

Now R-punzel was the cleverest child under the sun and could program in statistical packages before she could talk. When she was twelve years old, the witch shut her up in a tower, in the middle of a great wood, and the tower had neither stairs nor doors, only a small window at the very top.

When the old witch wanted to get in, she stood underneath and exercised a call option:

"R-punzel, R-punzel, throw down your golden ratio hair," for R-punzel had hair whose curve conformed to the golden spiral. Whenever she heard the witch's voice, she loosened her plaits, and let her hair fall down out of the window about twenty yards below, and the old witch climbed up by it.

But R-punzel was too clever by far, and often the witch wondered whether she was an asset or a liability. For example, R-punzel's modelling quickly pointed out the flaws in this story and she questioned the witch thus:

"Hair grows at an average of ½ inch per month, so by age 12 my hair will have grown by 6 feet. But the distance from the window to the ground is 20 yards – which is 10 times this distance. How can this be?"

The witch responded, "I'm a powerful witch and so can do things like that."

"But ignoring the fact that you climbing on my hair should cause it to rip from my scalp, my body mass at 12 wouldn't have been enough to offset your weight when you climbed and I would have fallen out the window."

"Err... you tied your hair around a solid object."

"OK, but still we're ignoring the issue of how I actually got into the tower in the first place?"

"I used my magical powers."

"But why don't you use those powers to get into the tower now instead of using my hair? Surely, this would imply that your powers are decaying over time."

"Shut up and just tell me how to increase the value of my investments."

"How can I shut up *and* tell you, as I don't know sign language?"

The witch glared at her.

R-punzel became frightened and hastily added, "Well, I'll apply a continuity correction to this story for now, but as an actuary, you should know that I can't abide known unknowns.

Anyway, I would recommend you stop investing in rampion and move into cryptocurrency. Though there is greater volatility that would seem to be well matched with your personality."

After they had lived like this for a few years, it happened one day that an actuarial prince was riding through the wood and passed by the tower. As he drew near it, he heard someone reciting sweet R code. He stood still, spell-bound, and listened. It was R-punzel in her little programming zone, letting her sweet voice ring out into the wood. Though, as an actuary, had she realised that anyone was listening, she would have been mortified.

The prince longed to see the owner of the voice, but he sought in vain for the tower door. Seeing none, he thought to scale the tower, but it was too smooth and his hands and feet couldn't find footholds that would be a good fit. So he applied scaled tower deviance to think of a different way of getting in. But he only got himself in a state for not remembering Markov's process for jumping so high!

If only he worked in reserving, he could construct a chain ladder to climb up, but he was in pricing and could only value her coding so much that he returned every day to the wood and listened.

One day, when he was standing behind a tree, he saw the old

witch approach and heard her call out:

"R-punzel, R-punzel, throw down your golden ratio hair."

Then R-punzel let her hair fall down, and the witch climbed up by it.

"So that's the staircase, is it?" said the prince. "Then I too will climb it and try my luck."

So on the following day, at dusk, he went to the foot of the tower and cried:

"R-punzel, R-punzel, *let down* your golden ratio hair."

But R-punzel replied, "I'm not letting down my hair for anyone! For I am a shy actuary who'd prefer a quiet night in the office running code."

The prince quickly realised his error and asked R-punzel to throw down her hair instead.

At first R-punzel was terribly frightened when a stranger came in to her working environment; but their interaction term was so significant to her generalised linear model that she felt like he was a natural parameter and she was soon chatting unselfconsciously. Soon, the prince offered her a position at his insurance business and her hand in marriage, for he declared that his life was a null model without her. R-punzel consented thus:

"Yes, I will gladly link function with you as long as you promise to include no small talk terms in our marriage model."

The prince gladly agreed, and they looked forward to starting an exponential family together. But first they set about working out how R-punzel was to escape the tower. "I know, every time you come to see me you must bring a transition matrix with you, and I will construct a Markov chain from them, and when it is finished, I will climb down by it, and you will take me away on your horse."

And so they set about their plan until the Markov chain was ready, but as she was climbing down, who should arrive unexpectedly but the old witch!

"Oh! You wicked actuary," cried the witch, for she knew that true actuaries never socialise. "I won't let you escape!"

But the prince had a set of actuarial tables with formulae in them. Quick as a flash, he displayed the page with Itô's Lemma and the witch cowered in fear long enough for them to make their getaway.

Then he led her to his kingdom, where they were welcomed with great joy, and they were predicted to live happily in 95% of their model's simulations over an ever after time horizon.

The 3 Little Actuarial Pigs

Data source

https://www.worldoftales.com/European_folktales/
English_folktale_104.html

Assumptions

- Pigs can become actuaries and construct statistical models.

- Outlier data point wolves prowl around looking for models built on poor assumptions.

- Huffing and puffing from outlier wolves destroys actuarial models with poor assumptions.

Once upon an ungrounded assumption, there were three little trainee actuary pigs, and each of their companies tasked them with building their very first model.

Now, as the first actuarial pig was wandering around the office, he met a man carrying a normality assumption. So he said very politely:

"If you please, sir, could you give me that assumption to build a model of log-returns on the stock market?"

And the man, seeing what good manners the little actuarial pig had (and being shocked that an actuary spoke to him in the first place) gave him the assumption, and the little actuary set to work and built a beautiful model with it. And it fitted all the data so well (once he had removed all the values that didn't conform to its assumptions).

Since normality was mathematically convenient, he finished constructing the model in no time. However, an outlier data point wolf (more than 3 standard deviations away from the mean) passed by that office, saw the model, and smelt the trainee actuarial pig who had built it. So the outlier wolf knocked at the model and said:

"Little actuary! Let me come in!"

But the little actuarial pig saw the extreme data point wolf which didn't fit his normal model and answered back:

"My assumptions say that's a big sin!"

Then the data point wolf showed his teeth and said:

"Then I'll huff and I'll puff and I'll blow your model in."

So he huffed, and he puffed, and the leptokurtic nature of investment returns blew the model in. The outlier wolf ate up the pride of the little trainee actuary, who then quit the Profession in shame.

And so the Kaplan-Meier estimate of the survival function of actuarial trainees' models dropped from 1 to 2/3.

Now, as the second actuarial pig was wandering around the office, he met a man carrying a last year's assumptions and experience adjustment. So he said very politely:

"If you please, sir, could you give me those assumptions to build a model of our pension liabilities?"

And the man, seeing what good manners the little actuarial pig had (and how the actuary conformed to actuarial best practice) gave him the assumptions and experience adjustment, and the little actuary set to work and built a beautiful model with it.

However, the outlier data point wolf passed by that office, saw the model, and smelt the trainee actuarial pig who had built it. So the outlier wolf knocked at the model and said:

"Little actuary! Let me come in!"

But the little actuarial pig saw that his past data did not predict this wolf's data point and answered back:

"My assumptions say that's a big sin!"

Then the outlier wolf showed his teeth and said:

"Then I'll huff and I'll puff and I'll blow your model in."

So he huffed, and he puffed, and the pandemic blew the model in. The outlier wolf ate up the pride of the little trainee actuary, who then quit the Profession in shame.

And so the Kaplan-Meier estimate of the survival function of actuarial trainees' models dropped from 2/3 to 1/3.

Now, as the third actuarial pig was wandering around the office, he met a man carrying Box's assumption that "all models are wrong but some are useful". So he said very politely:

"If you please, sir, could you give me that assumption to build a model that will expect a non-conforming data point?"

And the man, seeing what how the little actuarial pig had clearly been reading *The Actuary* magazine, gave him the assumption and the little actuary set to work and with much effort built a beautiful model based on it, which he had peer reviewed.

However, the outlier data point wolf passed by that office, saw the model, and smelt the trainee actuarial pig who had built it. So the outlier wolf knocked at the model and said:

"Little actuary! Let me come in!"

The little actuary saw the expected outlier wolf and answered back: "Sure, come on in."

And this mightily confused the data point, for if he went in, he would confirm the model's assumptions, which he clearly didn't want to do. But if he went away, then clearly he wouldn't be able to go in and break the model.

So, after much hesitation, the outlier wolf eventually went in to see if he could wreak havoc on the model from the inside. But the model *ate the outlier data point wolf* up, and the company promoted the trainee actuarial pig, which boosted his pride.

So the Kaplan-Meier estimate of the survival function of actuarial trainees' models remained at 1/3. And the trainee actuary would have lived happily ever after had he not then failed his next exam because he didn't have time to study whilst meeting his increased work responsibilities.

The Frogtuary Prince

Data source

https://www.worldoftales.com/fairy_tales/Brothers_Grimm/
Margaret_Hunt/The_Frog-King,_or_Iron_Henry.html

Assumptions

- Princesses are allowed to play on their own with golden balls next to deep wells in forests outside palaces.

- Actuaries appear frog-like to non-actuarial princesses.

- Princesses can overcome their revulsion and kiss actuaries if the actuaries turn into handsome young princes.

Once upon a hypothesis test, there lived a king who had three beautiful daughters. In the vicinity of the king's castle there was a dark forest, and in this forest, beneath an old binomial tree, there was a well.

In the heat of the day, the youngest princess would go out into the forest and sit on the edge of the cool well. To pass the time, she engaged in frivolous risk-seeking behaviour by throwing a golden ball into the air, and then attempting to catch it.

Now one day, the law of large numbers finally caught up with her and she missed catching the ball. It fell to the ground and, because of the pooling of risk, the ball rolled right into the water.

Horrified, the princess saw it sink down, and the well was so deep that she could not see its bottom.

Then the princess, who had myopic loss aversion, cried bitterly and issued a statement without proper due diligence or even a peer review, "I'd give anything, if only I could get my ball back: my clothes, my precious stones, my pearls, anything in the world."

At this, an actuary who had been seeking such an arbitrage opportunity appeared and said, "Princess, why are you crying so bitterly?"

"Oh," she said, "an actuary!"

Inwardly, she was repulsed by him as he reminded her of a slimy frog. "How can you help me get my golden ball back? It's practical help I need not... err... whatever it is that you do."

The frog actuary overlooked the insult as part of the systematic risk of his profession and replied, "I do not want your pearls or your precious stones as I'm an actuary with an excellent remuneration package, and I'm not really into cross dressing so keep your clothes. But if you'll be my girlfriend and even kiss me, then I'll bring your ball back to you."

The princess thought, "What is this stupid frog-like actuary trying to say? After all, all he does is calculations all day. Even so, maybe he can get my ball," and she said aloud, "Yes, for all I care. Just bring me back my golden ball, and I'll promise everything."

The mere thought of this overwhelmed the actuary, as he'd never had a girlfriend before, nor even a friend. So he immediately set to work.

First, he used the maximum likelihood of the princess's loss distribution to give the best estimate of its location. Since the ball was an asset to the princess, he then used an asset return model to find the optimal way of getting it back: insurance!

Fortunately, this actuary lived in the forest, as nobody in the castle or village enjoyed having him nearby, and since he was a risk averse actuary, he had insured the well and the water in it against accidental damage, including items being dropped in it.

He called upon his reinsurer, with whom he had an excess-of-loss treaty, to come and remove the excess water above the ball. It was then easy to extract the ball and return it to the princess.

When the princess picked up the ball, she was so happy to have it back again that she could think of nothing else than to run home with it (at least that's what she told the fairy tale writer).

The actuary called after her, "Wait, princess, take me with you like you promised," but the Vasicek model showed that her rate of interest in him had declined to near zero.

The actuary didn't lose heart though (possibly because actuaries don't have hearts). He simply took the princess's promise as IBNR and accepted it would appear in due time.

The next day the princess was sitting at the table with the king and all the people of the court, and was eating from her golden plate when there came a knock at the door, and a voice called out, "Princess, youngest, open the door for me!"

She ran and opened the door, presumably because they had

spent all their money on golden plates and balls and therefore had none left over for door servants.

It was the frog-like actuary, whom she had put completely out of her mind after the extensive PTSD counselling. Scared of the consequences of her rash promise, she slammed the door shut and returned to the table.

The king saw that her heart was pounding (presumably because kings have X-ray vision) and asked, "My child, why are you afraid? Is there an accountant outside the door who wishes to audit why we can't afford servants?"

"Oh, no," she answered. "It's worse than that – it's an ugly frog-like actuary."

"What does this actuary want from you?"

"He got my golden ball out of the water. I promised him that he could be my boyfriend and even kiss me. I didn't think that he would ever leave his social isolation to come and find me, but now he is just outside the door and wants to come in."

Just then, the actuary knocked and called out again. The king said, "What you have promised, you must keep, for as royals, our word is our bond."

"Can't my word have an optional redemption date?" she pouted. However, given the king's stern look, she obeyed.

The opportunity cost of having a girlfriend helped the actuary overcome his natural reticence, and so he followed her inside and sat down next to her for afternoon tea.

"Have I told you my favourite digits of pi?" asked the actuary conversationally.

"Oh, for F distribution's sake!" shouted the princess, to which the actuary calmly replied, "I think the t-distribution is more appropriate for this meal."

The princess fumed silently as the actuary carried on with his geeky one-sided conversation. The duration of afternoon tea was only 20 minutes, but the effective duration felt like a lifetime. If only she had enacted Redington's conditions of immunisation...

Eventually, the princess could stand it no longer. "Look, this'll never work, as we're just mismatched. I'm a beautiful and popular princess and you're ugly and despised."

"This means that we'd be a perfect diversified couple," the actuary excitedly replied.

The princess silently fumed some more.

The actuary enjoyed his meal, but for her, every bite stuck in her throat. Finally, he said, "Thank you for the meal. How about a kiss for your boyfriend?"

The princess was horrified when she heard this and began to cry. The king scolded her and said, "You should not despise someone who has helped you in time of need."

To help the princess overcome her revulsion, the actuary told her how he had been enchanted by a wicked witch, and that by kissing him, he would turn back into a handsome young prince.

The princess was encouraged by these words, but she'd still have to kiss an actuary. "Someone should pay me for this gross activity," she murmured.

"I suppose that since royalty doesn't pay taxes, it would actually be a gross premium," the actuary helpfully replied.

The princess braced herself and kissed the actuary. However, nothing happened.

"Don't reject my null hypothesis yet – it's simply a Type I error – 5% of kisses to princes enchanted by wicked witches have no effect. You just need to try again. Maybe we should to use a more powerful test – perhaps a French kiss?"

It was certainly the most testing time the princess had ever faced, but she kissed the actuary one more time.

Even so, there was no change.

"What's going on?" she demanded.

"Admittedly, the chance of this happening is 0.05^2, which is tiny, but it still happens. One more kiss should reduce this Type I error to almost zero..." he added hopefully.

"You're not actually a prince, are you?"

"Well... in my office they call me the prince of spreadsheets and so technically..."

He trailed off as he saw the venomous look on the princess's face.

"And I believed you!" she spat.

"Well, I have a high credibility factor which shifted your estimate of kissing me from your previous prior of zero towards the average of my sample of conversation..."

The glare silenced him once again.

"It's over," declared the princess.

"I'm sorry for the deception, but this was the only scenario in over 1,000,000 simulations from my modelling that had any positive chance of actuarial dating success."

The actuary headed to the door, "if you ever want someone to help minimise any future obligations incurred from rash promises, then you know where I can be found."

And although the non-actuarial world viewed his 30 minutes

of dating and two kisses as rather pathetic, this actuary's achievement became a legend that inspired hope in generations of actuaries ever after.

The 3 Bond Goats Gruff

Data source

https://www.worldoftales.com/European_folktales/
Norwegian_folktale_12.html

Assumptions

- Companies issue corporate bond goats.

- Credit rating trolls' utility function prefers bigger goats to smaller goats.

- Fairy tales use capital letters to indicate loud noises, long before Internet etiquette determined it should be so.

- The river of bond approval is wet.

Once upon an optional redemption date there were three corporate bond goats, who were all going to the financial markets to be purchased, and they were all three issued by the company Gruff Inc.

On the way to these markets, there was a bridge over the river of approval they had to cross; and under the bridge lived the great ugly Credit Rating Troll, with eyes as big as saucers, and a nose as long as a long-nosed thing.

So onto the bridge walked the littlest bond goat issued by Gruff Inc.

"Trip, trap! Trip, trap!" went the bridge, which was strange because bridges don't normally talk.

"Who's that trip trapping over my bridge?" roared the Credit Rating Troll.

"Oh! It is only I, the tiniest term bond goat issued by Gruff Inc. and I'm going to market," said the bond goat, with such a small voice.

"Now, I'm coming to gobble you up and give you junk status," said the troll.

"Oh, no! I'm far too short-term, hardly longer than cash assets really, with little liquidity risk..." said the littlest bond goat; "wait until the second bond goat issued by Gruff Inc. comes to market. He's got a 7-year term."

Under the non-satiation of the troll's utility function, he was naturally inclined to prefer a bigger bond goat over a smaller one and replied, "Well! Be off with you then."

Besides, he thought to himself, it's only proper that I collect more data so I'm able to carry out statistically meaningful analysis.

A little while later, the second bond goat issued by Gruff Inc. came to cross the bridge.

"Trip, trap! Trip, trap! Trip, trap!" went the bridge, which is still the most disturbing feature of this story. I mean, walking over a rickety wooden bridge over a deep chasm is bad enough, without it then talking to you.

"WHO'S THAT trip trapping over my bridge?" roared the Credit Rating Troll.

"Oh! It's the mid-term bond goat issued by Gruff Inc. and I'm going to market," said the bond goat, who hadn't such a small voice.

"Now, I'm coming to gobble you up and give you junk status," said the troll.

"Oh, no! Don't junk me - I know I'm a medium-term bond, but I have a high running yield..." he galloped across the bridge to demonstrate, "which offsets my volatility. Besides, if you wait a bit until the third bond goat issued by Gruff Inc. comes to market, he's got a whopping 15-year term."

The opportunity cost seemed too good to pass up, but the Credit Rating Troll wondered, "Are two goats enough to cause me to be influenced by herd bias?"

He decided not.

"Very well! Be off with you," said the Credit Troll.

But just then the third bond goat issued by Gruff Inc. came to cross the bridge.

"TRIP, TRAP! TRIP, TRAP! TRIP, TRAP!" went the bridge, for the bond goat had such a long term that the bridge creaked and groaned under him. Though it would have been probably more helpful if the bridge had said, "Get off me you big thing – you're hurting me!"

"WHO'S THAT tramping over my bridge?" roared the Credit Rating Troll.

"IT IS I! THE BIG TERM BOND GOAT," said the bond goat, who was volatile and very mean (well, he had a big discounted *mean* term).

"Now, I'm coming to gobble you up and give you junk status," roared the troll.

But only when he climbed onto the bridge did he realise that the expectations theory of his interest in the bond goat was very different to the reality.

For this was certainly not a subordinate bond goat, and the troll realised that his shortfall probability into the river was larger than he ever anticipated.

With one Cramér-Rao lower bound, the goat leapt on the troll and struck him head on and market segmented him into the air, away from the goat bonds.

As the troll was falling, he saw the back of the huge bond goat and realised he had suffered from behind sight bias.

Splash went the troll into the river below and the poor soaked troll was left wondering why investors ever had liquidity preference.

RumpelSTATSkin

Data source

https://www.worldoftales.com/fairy_tales/
Andrew_Lang_fairy_books/Blue_fairy_book/
Rumpelstiltzkin.html

Assumptions

- Millers have audiences with kings.

- Millers boast of their actuarial children's capabilities because they have no idea what they actually do.

- Kings greatly value actuarial models (though possibly because they confuse them with fashion models).

- Crying causes a grotesque little man to appear who can solve actuarial problems for a small fee.

- Kings believe that offers of marriage to girls they have treated appallingly will be accepted.

- The Actuarial Control Cycle can be used to obtain unusual names of grotesque little men.

Once upon an actuarial exam sitting, there lived a poor miller who had a daughter who was an actuary. Now it happened one day that he had an audience with the king, and in order to appear a person of some importance, he told the king that his daughter was such an amazing actuary she could construct models using straw instead of data.

"Now that's a talent worth having," said the king to the miller; "if your daughter is as clever as you say, bring her to my palace tomorrow, and I'll put her to the test."

When the girl was brought to him he led her into a room full of straw, gave her a copy of Excel, a writing pad and a pencil, and said: "Now set to work and use this straw to model my investment returns all night till early dawn, and if by that time you haven't found the strategy that maximises my returns you shall die." Then he closed the door behind him and left her alone inside.

So the poor miller's daughter sat down, and although she wasn't in Markov chains, she was certainly in a state, for she didn't know what in the world she was to do. She hadn't the least idea of how to model using straw instead of data and her force of transition into despair was high indeed.

Suddenly the door opened, and in stepped a tiny little man and said: "Good evening, Miss Miller-maid; why are you crying so bitterly?"

"Oh!" answered the girl, for it appeared that conversation was now to be added to her list of woes. "I have to model investment returns using straw instead of data, and haven't a notion how it's done."

"What will you give me if I construct the model for you?" asked the little man.

"My social life," replied the girl.

"Ha!" spat the little man, for he knew that this was of negligible value to an actuary. However, he signed her risk transfer agreement, sat himself down at Excel, and examining the straw, he started tapping away. So it went on till the morning, until each piece of straw had been examined, and the model had produced enough simulations to find the best investment strategy for the king.

As soon as the sun rose, the king came, and when he perceived the recommendation, he was astonished and delighted. But his heart only lusted more than ever after other statistical models (which is completely understandable to us actuaries).

He had the miller's daughter put into another room full of straw, much bigger than the first, and bade her, if she valued her life, to create a model that maximised his food production from his farmland before the following morning.

The girl didn't know what to do, but wondered if there was a correlation between her crying and the little man appearing. So she began to cry, and the door opened as before as the tiny little man walked in and said: "What will you give me if I use this straw to construct another model for you?"

The actuary saw another arbitrage opportunity and said, "My friends." The little man agreed (not yet realising how poor a deal he was being offered), and the sound of tapping on the keyboard began. When morning broke, he had used all the straw to model the various outcomes and come up with a strategy that would maximise the king's food production.

The king was pleased beyond measure at the sight of the audit trail in the spreadsheet, but his greed for statistical models was still not satisfied.

So he had the miller's daughter brought into a yet bigger room full of straw and said: "You must use this straw to construct a model that maximises my chances of beating my enemies in battle; but if you succeed this time, you shall become my wife."

"She's only an actuary, it's true," he thought; "but it'll make my remaining life seem so much longer if I marry a bore like her."

The girl was considering refusing, but realised that she was unlikely to find someone else who valued statistical models so much. The palace was also much larger than any other house, which maximised her chances of being alone.

When the king had left, the little man appeared for the third time and said: "What will you give me if I construct a model using the straw for you once again?"

"I've nothing more to give," answered the girl.

"Then promise that when you are queen, you will give me your actuarial tables on the birth of your first child."

The cheek!

Her tables were her lifetime's work, and their value was beyond compare. However, she thought, "There is no risk that can't be hedged via a suitable derivative." So she promised the creature what he demanded, and he set to work once more and produced his finest model yet, using straw instead of data.

When the king came in the morning, and found everything as he had desired, he immediately married her, and the miller's daughter became the queen.

When a year had passed, a beautiful son was born to her, and the little man stepped into her room and said: "Now give me what you promised."

The queen calmly produced her derivative contract. But the

little man said: "Ha, you neglected to hedge against counterparty risk for this company recently went bankrupt!"

Then the queen began to cry and sob so bitterly that the little man became sorry for her, and said: "I'll give you three days to guess my name, and if you find it out in that time you may keep your actuarial tables."

So the queen spent the entire night using the Actuarial Control Cycle to solve this problem. After checking the regulations on guessing names, she discovered that there was no limit to the number of names she could give. So she developed a simple solution based on the assumption that it was a common name: collect all the names of everyone in the land and regurgitate them as fast as possible.

She sent a messenger to scour the land and note any names he came across. When the little man arrived the following day, she reeled through the list of names that had been compiled, but at each one the little man replied: "That's not my name."

Clearly, these actual results were not what she had expected. So she revised her assumption to include unusual names and also used simulation to create alternative names based on a convolution of common names. However, to each of these strange names he always replied: "That's not my name."

Assuming that the little man was following the actuaries' code and was acting with integrity, she realised that monitoring the little man rather than the outcomes could solve this problem.

On the third day a messenger returned and announced: "I saw the grotesque little man in the wood hopping on one leg around a fire crying: 'Tomorrow a model I'll make, for then the tables away I'll take; for the royal dame does not guess that Rumpelstatskin is my name!'"

You can imagine the queen's delight at successfully solving this problem and when the little man stepped in shortly afterward and asked: "Now, my lady queen, what's my name?" she answered "Is your name perhaps, Rumpelstatskin?"

"Some statistician told you that!" screamed the little man and in his rage, he tore himself into two homogenous subgroups.

Which made for a rather abrupt ending to the story.

The 3 Actuarial Wishes

Data source

https://www.worldoftales.com/European_folktales/
English_folktale_65.html

Assumptions

- Financial reporting fairies exist.

- The aforementioned fairies offer wishes in return for kind acts.

- Actuaries should always undertake a thorough risk analysis before making any wishes.

- All the wishes in the world can't solve the fundamental actuarial dilemma.

Once upon a repetitive fairy tale opening phrase, there was a poor student on a summer actuarial internship.

His day was filled with the grunt work that the real actuaries didn't want to do. So he scanned documents, formatted presentations, cleaned up data and modified spreadsheets to make their lives easier.

But one day as he opened up an ancient presentation there appeared a fairy.

"I am the financial reporting fairy and make my home in this PowerPoint '97 file."

And with that, the fairy prayed and beseeched him to spare the file from updating.

He was stunned and couldn't open his mouth to utter a single word, though this is not unusual for those that seek to become actuaries. However, after quickly carrying out an initial appraisal of this strange request, he saw that the risk was minimal, and there might be a large upside potential by doing what the fairy asked. He found his tongue at last, and replied, "I'll do as you have asked."

"You've done better for yourself than you know," answered the fairy, "and to show I'm not ungrateful, I'll grant you your next three wishes, be they what they may."

And with that, the fairy was no more to be seen, and so the student went home at the end of that day to tell his wife the good news.

She was overjoyed when she heard. Well, technically she was just Joy, for that was her name. "Let's plan the best way to use this scarce resource to make our lives better," she said.

"Surely, we could just wish for more wishes," said he.

"Everyone knows that kind of wish arbitrage is forbidden by the fairy regulator. And please stop calling me Shirley."

"How about a lifetime annuity?" said he.

"You really are cut out for the boring actuarial life," said she, "but frankly you're also too actuarial to have any happiness unless you're working at least 12 hours a day."

He nodded at that. "Perhaps the best way to select the three variables that would maximise our future happiness would be to start with everything we ever wanted and use backward selection to remove those items that are insignificant to our overall joy."

"That would just take too long. It'll be much simpler to use forward selection and start with the best wish that will reduce our current unhappiness."

"Obviously that would be getting a proper job after this

internship, but I'm struggling to do the work I'm given, and study for the exams, let alone have any kind of social life!"

"There you have it then," she declared. "Let's wish that you'll be able to do all the work, so you get offered a job!"

His first wish was made, and immediately he could do all the grunt work they assigned him and they soon offered him a permanent position.

But despite him being able to do all the work, he hadn't anticipated that this would be at the expense of his time to study and he failed the next set of exams that he sat.

"This is no good – sure they're impressed by my work, but they will not keep on employing me if I keep failing. Besides, passing more exams will increase my pay and surely our happiness."

His wife agreed and so, after a thorough risk analysis, he wished he could do all his work *and* be able to pass his exams.

And it was so! Soon he was passing his exams and getting pay rises and doing so well at work that he was promoted.

Life was going so well, except his wife became increasingly angry as she monitored the experience. He spent nearly all day in the office, and when he was at home, he was studying!

"I can't do this anymore – you might be happy, but I'm

miserable – if you don't wish that you can fit in some time with me, then I'm going to change my name from Joy to 'I'm leaving you'."

It was true – his second wish meant his actuarial life was perfect for him. But the lack of a social life meant that he had damaged his marriage almost beyond repair. So he quickly wished that he could have more time with his wife, without carrying out the due diligence such a wish required.

Immediately, a financial crash swept the world, and he soon found himself unemployed. Whilst he now had plenty of time to spend with his wife and to study for his final exams, the sudden lack of money meant they couldn't actually afford to do anything, which didn't seem to satisfy his wife either.

And the moral of this story is that actuaries can't have it all, even with wishes.

Snow Actuary and the Diversified Portfolio of Dwarves

Data source

https://www.worldoftales.com/fairy_tales/Brothers_Grimm/
Margaret_Hunt/Little_Snow-white.html

Assumptions

- Step mothers are statistically more likely to exhibit personality flaws.

- Magic mirrors answer questions truthfully.

- Dwarves are happy to live with actuaries (if only so they can increase the value of their investments).

- Princes have a penchant for wandering in woods and coming upon damsels in distress.

- Princes are happy to marry actuaries (if only so they can increase the value of their investments).

Once upon an investment return, there lived a queen who longed for an actuarial child (because, let's be honest, who wouldn't want one), and it grieved her sorely that she didn't have one. But eventually, she gave birth to a little daughter who was as clever as clever can be (and that's pretty clever, let me tell you).

However, despite the child's mental acuity, her personality was rather frozen (because as actuaries know, brains and personality are mutually exclusive) and so they called her Snow Actuary.

But sadly, her kind-hearted mother at age 39 last birthday, felt sorry that q_{39} was less than 0.1% and helped it out by dying. Her father soon remarried again; a rich investment banker, and spent the rest of his life saying "correlation is not causation" to anyone who said he only married her for the money.

However, Snow Actuary's step mother was insanely competitive (because, let's face it, a Cox proportional hazard model would clearly show that step-mothers in fairy tales are at least five times more likely to possess major character flaws). And so every morning the queen would stand before her fairy mirror and say:

"Mirror, mirror, on the wall, whose fund is the greatest of all?"

(Because spreadsheets and the internet hadn't been invented yet, and so calculating the value of a volatile fund was tricky to do without magical help).

And the mirror always used to reply:

"Queen, queen, on thy throne, the greatest portfolio is thine alone." (Because after a bit of flattery, genuine magical items always speak in Olde English, not like those cheap counterfeits you get down the market).

Then she was quite happy, for she knew the mirror always spoke the truth (at least that's what the fairy who sold it to her said).

But Snow Actuary grew cleverer and cleverer every year and soon was leveraging derivatives to grow her investment fund until at last one day the mirror replied:

"Queen, queen, on thy throne, Snow Actuary's fund is greater than thy own."

Then the queen turned green in her jealousy (though it was probably something she ate, given that they didn't have refrigeration in those days).

She called a servant and said, "Take the actuarial child into a busy public place that will be sure to be the death of her, and bring me back her actuarial tables that I may know for certain she is dead." (Because everyone knows no one can willingly part actuaries from their tables while they're alive. And to be fair, rigor mortis also makes it quite hard to part actuaries from their tables when they're dead).

But when the servant had taken Snow Actuary out into a public place, he saw the look on her face like a rabbit caught in the headlights (except that headlights and cars hadn't been invented yet, so this momentary lapse in the servant's language revealed his secret identity as somebody from the future) and had pity on her (though to be fair, most people have pity on actuaries because of their lack of personality. This pity usually lasts right until the point where they find out how much actuaries earn).

So he let Snow Actuary run off and purchased a new set of actuarial tables from the Profession to give to the queen. However, the three-month delay before they eventually arrived was tricky to explain except by smacking himself over the head and claiming amnesia.

Snow Actuary ran as far as her legs would carry her, which wasn't very far at all, because actuaries stay chained to their desks all day and get little exercise apart from the finger that presses F9 on the keyboard.

Conveniently, there was a mountain hut nearby, and she knocked at the door, but got no reply. So she lifted the latch and walked in. (This poor behaviour was clearly because of the influence of her Sales & Marketing Tutor).

When the dwarves returned to their hut, they saw Snow Actuary sleeping in a bed with her actuarial tables beside her and exclaimed, "Oh, heavens! What a clever child!"

When it was morning, Snow Actuary awoke and, upon seeing the dwarves, was glad that she'd taken out microinsurance which protected her against small people.

She quickly used her presentation skills (learned from the actuarial communication exam) to explain how the queen's jealously of her portfolio meant Snow Actuary had to flee to avoid being killed.

Then the dwarves asked if she would stay with them and invest their gold to make a good return. She readily agreed once she found out that she'd be alone during most of the day while the dwarves were digging for gold in the mountains.

But the dwarfs, who enjoyed stating the obvious, warned her, "Beware the queen, for she will soon know that you are here, so don't let anyone in the house."

Snow Actuary answered, "Hey, I'm an actuary; I've so got that covered."

Next morning the queen went to her mirror as usual and

asked:

"Mirror, mirror, on the wall, whose fund is the greatest of all?"

But the mirror answered, "Queen, queen, on thy throne, Snow Actuary's fund is still greater than thy own."

When the queen heard these words, she realised either the mirror was lying or her servant was lying, or both were lying (as these statements are not mutually exclusive).

A quick dose of stochastic calculus and the servant confessed all. So she made him use a binary search of the forest until he found Snow Actuary and informed the queen.

The queen pondered day and night (though not at the same time as these *are* definitely mutually exclusive) how she might destroy Snow Actuary's fund until she hit upon a plan.

The queen disguised herself as an old financial analyst woman and went to the hut and knocked at the door, calling out:

"Cryptocurrency for sale, cryptocurrency for sale!"

Snow Actuary couldn't believe her luck, as she couldn't leave the hut to get to the nearest trading floor and the internet was pretty temperamental given that it hadn't been invented yet.

But Snow White promised the dwarves that she wouldn't let

anyone in the house, but that didn't include her stepping outside briefly.

"Hello there, my good woman, what have you to sell?"

"All kinds of cryptocurrency: Dogecoin, Ethereum, and Litecoin. Buy them while they're cheap!"

This seemed like a great opportunity to purchase undervalued stock before the rest of the market caught on. So Snow Actuary sold most of the dwarves' gold and purchased almost two Bitcoins.

But no sooner had Snow Actuary purchased them that their value plummeted, and she collapsed in shock.

"Now my fund is the greatest," said the queen to herself as she ran away.

When the dwarfs came home that evening, they found Snow Actuary lying upon the ground as if she were dead (rather like actuaries appear during a trustee meeting). One dwarf moved her actuarial tables, and she suddenly revived and immediately set up a long straddle on Bitcoin's price and began profiting from the extreme volatility of cryptocurrency until her fund was greater than before.

When the diversified portfolio of dwarves heard what had happened, they said, "That old financial analyst was none other than the wicked queen. In the future, you must be sure not to let anyone in *nor* go out to meet anyone."

The next morning the queen went to the mirror on the wall and said to it:

"Mirror, mirror, on the wall, whose fund is the greatest of all?"

But the mirror answered, "Queen, queen, on thy throne, Snow Actuary's fund is still greater than thy own."

When the queen heard that, she knew that Snow Actuary had outwitted her. She disguised herself as a different old financial analyst and went again to the hut and knocked at the door, calling out:

"Subprime mortgage-backed securities for sale!"

But Snow White promised the dwarves that she wouldn't let anyone in the house, nor go out to meet anyone, but these restrictions didn't preclude her from opening the door and trading across its threshold (and this clearly demonstrates why principles based regulation is superior to rules based regulation).

"Hello there, my good woman, what have you to sell?"

"Subprime mortgage-backed securities which offer great returns and they're currently rated AAA by reputable credit rating agencies."

This seemed too good to be true (and actuaries know their lives are never that good) so she was cautious about investing. Then the old woman said, "Tell you what, why don't we each purchase half of these securities?"

So the queen persuaded Snow Actuary to sell much of her portfolio and purchase these MBOs. However, little did she realise the queen had kept the first tranche for herself and sold Snow Actuary the remaining tranches.

As the subprime market collapsed, the value of these securities plummeted to zero with no opportunity to sell them. Snow White fell down as if dead in shock.

The queen, who smugly thought she would be fine, soon found out that her tranche also became worthless, and she too fell down dead in shock.

The dwarfs, when they came home in the evening, could not revive Snow Actuary by taking her actuarial tables or even by saying accountants are better than actuaries.

However, a prince came into the forest, (because there's a near perfect correlation between fairy tales and princes wandering in woods) and he saw Snow Actuary lying there and his heart was deeply moved (but fortunately his heart remained attached within his body or it could have been quite nasty).

He immediately enacted a government bailout for poor people like Snow Actuary (to be fair, she was poor now after her fund had collapsed).

Upon hearing this news, Snow Actuary revived and was married to the prince (because this story has really gone on long enough), and their joint fund grew happily ever after.

Beauty & the Beastly Actuary

Data source

https://www.gutenberg.org/files/26019/26019-h/
26019-h.htm#BEAUTY_AND_THE_BEAST

Assumptions

- Merchants often have three daughters and go on long journeys.

- Geeky children often ask their parents for equations.

- Prolonged exposure to actuaries can reduce standards.

- Magicians often curse people to become actuaries. Only a maiden can break such a curse by falling in love with the aforementioned actuary.

- No maiden has ever done so without payment.

Once upon a finite time period, a merchant had three daughters. Though let's be honest, a merchant having three daughters is probably quite common and so any decent actuarial model would predict this to have occurred more than once in any reasonable time period considered.

Anyway, one day he had to go on a long journey, though again it was probably more than once that this happened. However, the variance in this particular journey's events compared to the other journeys was very high.

As he was leaving, he asked his daughters, "What shall I bring you back, my dears?"

And they replied, "Dad, we're girls not deers!" For they were clearly unaware that deer was already plural.

Then the eldest daughter asked to have a necklace, for she valued beauty; the middle daughter wished for an influencer kit, for she valued fame; but the youngest said, "Bring back yourself, Papa, for that is what I want the most." For she valued being nauseating.

Her father gave her *that* look and so she relented, "then bring me back an equation, father, preferably one with an irrational number in it." For she was rather geeky like that.

Well, the merchant easily found the necklace and influencer kit, but he found no traders selling equations because, let's be honest, there is little market for them.

However, as he was nearing home, he passed a magnificent house and pinned on boards outside were various equations. So he got off his horse and wandered about the boards until he found an interesting looking one called the "Black-Scholes equation". And so he unpinned it from the board, rolled it up and headed back to his horse.

At that moment he heard dull monotonic voice intone, "Man, with expected future lifetime of 38 years (which might fall significantly depending on your answer), who said you could take one of my equations?"

The merchant turned and saw the most terrible sight, a beastly actuary wearing a grey suit (due to fear of being mistaken for an extrovert), with a face that was as pale as the moon (due to lack of sunlight), deep set bags under his eyes (because of working late at the office) and an unpleasant odour (due to skipping showers to fit in more study time).

The beast lurched towards the merchant armed with a set of actuarial tables and a mechanical pencil.

"Explain why your force of mortality shouldn't rapidly increase after stealing one of the ten mathematical equations that changed the world (according to an article on LinkedIn)," droned the beastly actuary.

"Please, sir," said the merchant in fear of falling into a coma from boredom, "I promised my geeky daughter to bring her home an equation and could find none anywhere save here and I thought you would not miss a single equation, or else I would have asked your permission."

"Breaking the actuaries' Code of Conduct is the most heinous of crimes," spat the Beastly Actuary, "and so your life is forfeit."

The merchant fell on his knees and begged for his life for the sake of his three daughters, who had none but him to support them.

The Beastly Actuary was caught off guard by the public display of emotion and replied, "Well, for the strike price of that equation you can either write me a 7 day call option on your life or on your youngest daughter staying here forever."

"Are they American or European options?"

"I can't abide uncertainty, so let it be a European option. So you have exactly 7 days to make your decision."

So the merchant signed the option for the Beastly Actuary to call upon his youngest daughter seven days hence. And taking his equation, he mounted his horse and rode home.

He distributed his gifts to his daughters, who were overjoyed, but the youngest asked, "Why did you sigh so deeply when you gave me my equation? Does not mathematics fill your heart with joy?"

"Bella, do you love your father?"

"Of course I do, Father, of course I do."

"Well, you won't when I tell you what I've signed you up for..."

Then he told her of all that had occurred with the Beastly Actuary when he got the equation for her. Her father's actions mightily peeved Bella but being the heroine of this fairy tale, she took it on the chin.

"Oh, Father, it was all on account of my geekiness that caused you to fall foul of this Beastly Actuary; so I will accept the terms of this call option."

So on the seventh day, Bella went to the Beastly Actuary's dwelling and bade her father farewell.

"No harm shall befall thee save that which is common to all those who come into close contact with actuaries," promised the Beastly Actuary.

So Bella lived in the home with the Beastly Actuary and whilst the beast let her use the *principle of correspondence* to write to her family every week, she was daily exposed to the risk of becoming bored senseless as he waxed lyrical about the joy of statistics.

She used *graduation* to slowly erode his crude nature, though his *Ornstein-Uhlenbeck* personality process meant he kept reverting to being mean, but the fact that she showed an interest in the beast's work clearly affected the actuary.

However, it was not just the beast that was being transformed, but Bella too, for her standards had begun to fall and she got to quite like him until one day the Beastly Actuary did not come at his usual time, and Bella missed him dearly.

So she wandered about the house, calling out his name, but received no reply. At last she found him huddled lifeless under the place from which her father had taken the equation. Then Bella was sorry indeed and remembered all the equations that the Beastly Actuary had talked to her about; and she threw herself down upon him weeping, "Oh, Beastly Actuary, why did you die? I was getting to love you so much."

No sooner had she said this than he transitioned from the "actuary" state into the "handsome young prince" state.

The prince rose and told her that a magician had cursed him to remain an actuary unless a maiden should, of her own accord, declare that she loved him.

"Of course, the magician had meant this curse to be forever, since this condition was never likely to be satisfied, so I owe you a debt of gratitude."

"We're to be married?" asked Bella excitedly.

"Not likely!" retorted the prince, "I mean, what prince worth his salt would marry someone with such poor taste?"

And so Bella was sent packing, with nothing but a lump sum of money for her troubles.

And the prince lived happily ever after marrying someone normal who had no interest in mathematics, whereas Bella lived daily exposed to longevity risk, as she didn't purchase an annuity with her lump sum.

Actuella

Data source

https://www.worldoftales.com/fairy_tales/
Andrew_Lang_fairy_books/Blue_fairy_book/
Cinderella,_or_the_Little_Glass_Slipper.html

Assumptions

- Widowers have poor taste in second wives who then become rubbish step mothers to their children.

- Actuaries would, with 99% confidence, rather stay at home than go to a ball.

- Actuarial godmothers appear to all good actuaries to rescue them from their social awkwardness.

- Magically created stationery works just as well as normal stationery.

- Actuella can run whilst wearing only one shoe.

- Female shoe sizes in the Kingdom are normally distributed.

Once upon a cashflow, a man who had a mathematical daughter remarried and, as any fairy tale statistical model will tell you, the probability a wife has personality issues given that she's the second wife is almost certain.

In this woman's case, she was the proudest and most vacuous woman, and her two daughters were likewise. So, for modelling purposes, these three women could be treated as a homogeneous group with the same risk profile.

As soon as they were married, his new wife showed her true risk profile, and the man realised he should have included an anti-selection mitigation clause in his wedding vows.

Now the step-function mother could not bear the fact that the man's daughter was most clever at mathematics, which made her own daughters appear even more stupid than they were. So the step-function mother said, "Seeing as you're so good at spreadsheets you can spread the sheets on our beds, and all the other tasks we are too important to do."

The step-function mother laughed at this rather sad pun that has been overused ever since actuaries first started using spreadsheets.

And the girl did it, for the step-function mother's patience had a short tail, whereas her temper had a fat tail and besides, *mean* people always make the laws (hence the "law of averages").

Finally, when the poor girl had completed her mind-numbing work, she used to sit in a quiet corner to manipulate data and she'd dream of becoming a fully qualified actuary and hitting F9 for a living. So her step-function sisters called her Actuella.

Now, the king gave a ball for his son, "the shy prince", and invited all persons of fashion to it, including the young misses because the king used a one-factor model that considered looks, but treated personality as an unimportant residual, and this fitted the step-sisters perfectly.

While they were getting Actuella to help them get ready, they asked, "Actuella, would you not like to go to the ball?"

"Not likely!" said she, "principal components analysis would reduce it to food, fluid and faff. The first two don't compensate for the negative present value of the third. I'd sooner attend a four hour spending review meeting!"

"But with so many people there, think of all the data you'd be missing out on," they mocked.

"I'd rather not be exposed to the risk of inane conversation," replied Actuella, "and with so many people there'd be a concentration of that risk that couldn't be easily mitigated."

When they told their mother about this, she saw an opportunity to humiliate the all-too-clever Actuella and declared, "Actuella *shall* go to the ball *and* wear a dress!"

At last the day came, and they all went to court, with poor Actuella muttering under her breath about the illogicality of a ball being called a ball given that it wasn't even spherical...

The ball was worse than her prospective reserving model predicted (for she was reserved and stood quietly to the side, studying for her next exam).

However, she had simply not expected that a discrete stream of people would come up to her and ask, "So what do you want to do when you grow up?"

Each time she'd answer "an actuary" even though she knew it would be a waste of her study time.

"Is that where they bury actors?" replied one.

"So you're good with the bow and arrow then?" replied another.

"Is that like an accountant?" replied the latest who shortly added, "Hey, why did you hit me?" after Actuella gave them the only sensible response to that question.

In the end, she could take it no more and ran to the ladies' room, where she burst into tears.

Her actuarial godmother, who saw her all in tears, said to her, "You wish with 95% confidence that you could escape the ball; is it not so?"

"Yes," cried Actuella, with a heaving sob.

"Well," said her godmother, "I will contrive that you shall leave." Then she said to her, "Run into the ballroom, and bring me a glass of wine, one of those pastries and a piece of fruit."

Cinderella gathered these items and brought them to her actuarial godmother, not being able to imagine how these could help her escape the ball. Her godmother used a series of swaps to exchange the wine for a set of actuarial tables, the pastry for a calculator and the fruit for a pencil and paper.

Having done this, she executed a forward contract with Uber to have someone come and pick her up. "Oh, thank you," cried Actuella; "but must I go wait outside in these fancy clothes?"

Her godmother then touched her with her generator function

wand, which reduced her back to business attire. This done, she gave Actuella a pair of comfortable work shoes.

Her godmother warned her, "I've given you a contingency margin of 10 minutes to get yourself to the gate outside. Don't be late or the Uber ride will leave you at the ball!" Actuella promised her godmother that she'd easily get to the kerb within 10 minutes and ran off, scarcely able to contain herself for joy.

As she exited the ballroom and headed down the garden, she bumped into a young man and dropped her tables. Being a gentleman, he picked them up and handed them back to her, adding, "A set of actuarial tables, so wonderful! Do you use them for calculating mortality rates and insurance premiums?"

Actuella was taken aback to have met someone who actually knew something about what she loved that she excitedly replied before she even realised that she was voluntarily entering conversation, "Mostly life premiums."

"I would have loved to have become an actuary. I could think of nothing more exciting than calculating all day," he sighed before adding, "But my father insists a prince should be interested in hunting and jousting."

"I'm so sorry," Actuella replied and put a hand on his shoulder to comfort him.

Then she mentally completed her regression on his complete sentence data, "Sorry, prince?"

"Yes, I'm afraid so. I'm so-called the 'shy prince' who'd rather be in the garden thinking about how to calculate all that I observe in the kingdom than being in a ball having boring conversations with empty-headed lords and ladies whilst wondering how quickly my future life expectancy..."

"... is heading to zero," finished Actuella, surprised that she found someone so similar to her, given that her personality was unusual and the sample size at the ball was small.

The prince smiled the most radiant smile and asked, "I don't suppose you'd like to..."

BEEP BEEP!

"The Uber ride!" gasped Actuella too late as the threshold exceedance was now over 10 seconds. "I'm really sorry, I've got to go."

"But..." the prince trailed off, for Actuella sprinted off in such haste that she dropped one of her sensible work shoes. The prince followed, picked up the shoe, but could not overtake her (possibly because carrying a shoe impeded his running ability, at least that's the excuse he used).

Later that evening, Actuella's step-sisters returned home full of gossip. "If you'd hadn't had spent most of your time hiding in the ladies' room before leaving early you would have heard that the prince was inconsolable after suffering an excess of loss when the 'most delightful woman he ever met' ran away but left behind the comfiest work shoe known to mankind."

What they said was very true; for a few days later, the king's son had it proclaimed, by sound of trumpet, that he would use the shoe and a chi-squared goodness-of-fit test to find the woman he was to marry.

Eventually, the two step-function sisters had their turn to try on the shoe. The first found that it fitted her. "I'm to be married to the prince!" she exclaimed. But the second grabbed the shoe off her and found it fitted her too! "No, *I'm* to marry the prince!"

Actuella, who saw this, sighed and said, "Female shoe sizes are normally distributed with a mean of size 6 and a standard deviation of 1.71. Given that the shoe is size 5 it will fit approximately 28.0% of the population!"

It was then that the servant exclaimed, "You're the one whom the prince wishes to marry! For he said, whoever complains about the size of the Type II error is surely the actuarial girl."

Her two sisters were astonished, and they threw themselves at Actuella's feet to beg pardon for all the ill treatment they had made her undergo lest she sought payback.

Actuella assured them she had such a high internal rate of return that her discounted payback period was zero. In fact, she invited them to lodge in the palace, so they could do all the small talk instead of her and the prince.

And the prince and Actuella married and the net present value of their future happiness was positive ever after.

The Residuals

Plot summaries of fairy tales whose low joke to story ratio didn't fit the humour model.

Jack Actuary and the Beanstalk

Data source

https://www.worldoftales.com/fairy_tales/
Andrew_Lang_fairy_books/Red_fairy_book/
Jack_and_the_Beanstalk.html

Key assumptions

- Poor actuaries are able to make surprisingly good trades when they sell the last of their possessions.

- Hens that lays golden eggs exist, but nobody ever mentions that they still need mucking out.

Synopsis

A poor actuarial intern sells his last bit of social life in return for some "worthless" actuarial flashcards that grow into a beautiful exam pass and untold riches from salary increases.

Pinocchio

Data source

https://www.gutenberg.org/files/500/500-h/500-h.htm

Key assumptions

- There exist puppets that can operate independently of their creators.

- Such puppets can talk, pass the Turing test and carry out actuarial calculations.

Synopsis

The story of an actuary with a wooden personality who longs to have a real life outside the office, but his ~~nose~~ project grows longer every time he has a free evening.

Puss in Boots

Data source

https://www.worldoftales.com/fairy_tales/
Andrew_Lang_fairy_books/Blue_fairy_book/
The_Master_Cat_or,_Puss_in_Boots.html

Key assumptions

- There exist boots that can fit small cats.

- Cats can walk around on two legs, talk to people and do something other than napping and judging humans.

Synopsis

A story about CAT modelling[5] some leather boots.

The cat then uses the bootstrapping statistical technique to lift himself and his master out of their poverty caused by an extreme event.

---

[5] CAT modelling is short for catastrophe modelling.

The Emperor's New Clothes

Data source

https://www.worldoftales.com/fairy_tales/

Hans_Christian_Andersen/Andersen_fairy_tale_48.html

Key assumptions

- Emperors have a convex utility function and desperately prefer more to less.

- Emperors therefore engage in risk-seeking behaviour to increase their utility.

Synopsis

One man's ego leaves him exposed to the risk of looking foolish by a *naked call* from a young boy.

The Little Red Actuarial Hen

Data source

https://americanliterature.com/childrens-stories/
the-little-red-hen

Key assumptions

- Hens are little and red and can train to become actuaries.

- The actuarial exams do not weed out lazy employees.

Synopsis

A trainee actuarial hen is preparing for a meeting with senior
management and no-one else in the office will help. But they
all want to take credit in the meeting.

The Pied Piper

Data source

https://www.worldoftales.com/European_folktales/
English_folktale_44.html

Key assumptions

- Fund managers can play the flute.

Synopsis

A story about how investors had all their assets taken away by
a fund manager with huge fees.

The Ugly Deductling

Data source
https://www.worldoftales.com/fairy_tales/
Hans_Christian_Andersen/Andersen_fairy_tale_3.html

Key assumptions
- Baby actuaries differ from non-actuarial babies.

- Non-actuaries tease actuaries because they are trying to cover up their mathematical insecurities.

Synopsis
A mother has five beautiful deductlings, all outgoing, and a very plain sixth one, who was quiet and withdrawn.

They all made fun of the quiet one because he was good at mathematics. But then one day he became a beautiful actuary and out earned them all.

The Little Actuarial Mermaid

Data source

https://www.worldoftales.com/fairy_tales/
Hans_Christian_Andersen/Andersen_fairy_tale_31.html

Key assumptions

- Princes have a significant effect on transition rates of mermaids.

- Witches are able to create potions that remove a mermaid's coefficient of lower tail dependency.

Synopsis

An actuary in the mermaid state of a Markov chain lives under the sea, swimming with the *Black Scholes* of fish.

However, after rescuing a prince from a shipwreck, she sees an opportunity to increase her net present value of future happiness by transitioning to the human state, even considering her expected tail loss.

And They Lived Happily Ever After

Heart-warming fairy tales especially created for you, the reader, out of the goodness of the author's heart with no ulterior motive at all.

Honest.

The Kind-Hearted Reader

Once upon a present moment, a reader wondered how they could encourage John to write more books, if only to keep him occupied and thus away from the public as long as possible.

And then the actuarial godmother appeared to the reader and told them she would be bless them with a social life if only they were to write a review about this book.

And then she waved her wand and a link to this book's Amazon page appeared:

getBook.at/ActuarialFairyTales

And the reader typed it in, wrote a review, and lived as happily as an actuary with friends might, given that social norms dictate they must talk to each other at least occasionally.

The Reader
Who Wanted More

Once upon a rift in the space-time continuum, there was a reader who finished this book and wanted more of the same. However, the reader denied it was merely to distract them from their sad actuarial life.

Statistical models recommended that the best fit solution to this problem involved the reader purchasing one of John's other comedy books:

Confessions of an Actuarial Tutor

The Ultimate Actuarial Joke Book

The Ultimate Actuarial Colouring Book

But then the reader finished those books and found the waiting time until the next book unbearable and longed for a regular annuity of actuarial/mathematical/Excel memes.

As if by magic the address of John's substack where he posts such jokes and offers subscribers discounts on his future books appeared on the line below:

actuarialtutor.substack.com

And the reader lived happily ever after until their p_x became 0.

The Author Who Wrote About Himself in the Third Person

Once upon a time, a child was born at a very young age with his umbilical cord wrapped around his neck. At first, it appeared that no lasting damage had been done, but as he grew, it became clear that his sense of humour had been damaged irreparably.

And his parents named him John, for they deemed it suitably boring enough to qualify as a "proper" actuarial name. And John grew up and studied mathematics at Oxford but still referred to himself in the third person.

Whilst there, he performed stand-up comedy as part of the Oxford Revue but took a wrong turn and ended up teaching actuaries who laugh little, except at accountants.

Now, when John is not wrestling with his work-life balance or literally wrestling with his four children, he's wrestling with writing funny words on a page in his cramped study.

John lives with his family near Oxford, England, where he wonders how his wife still finds the same jokes funny after more than 25 years of marriage.

And the reader lived happily ever after...

... though correlation between this book ending and the reader living happily should not be seen as causation.

Honest.

Printed in Great Britain
by Amazon